Laws of Association Football

C000120016

Guide for Players and Referees 1997–1998

Laws of Association Football

Guide for Players and Referees 1997–1998

Authorized by the International Football Association Board

Revised edition from 1 July 1997

PAN BOOKS

This edition published 1997 by Pan Books
an imprint of Macmillan Publishers Ltd
25 Eccleston Place, London, SW1W 9NF
and Basingstoke

Associated companies throughout the world

ISBN 0 330 352431

Copyright © Fedération Internationale de Football Association 1997, Hitzigweg 11, 8030 Zurich,
Switzerland
Additional material © The Football Association 1997, 16 Lancaster Gate, London W2 3LW

9 8 7 6 5 4 3 2 1

A CIP catalogue record for this book is available
from the British Library

Phototypeset by Intype London Ltd
Printed and bound in Great Britain
by Mackays of Chatham PLC

Notes on The Laws of the Game

Modifications

Subject to the agreement of the national association concerned and provided the principles of these Laws are maintained, the Laws may be modified in their application for matches for players of under 16 years of age, for women footballers and for veteran footballers (over 35 years).

Any or all of the following modifications are permissible:

- *size of the field of play*
- *size, weight and material of the ball*
- *width between the goalposts and height of the crossbar from the ground*
- *the duration of the periods of play*
- *number of substitutions*

Further modifications are only allowed with the consent of the International Football Association Board.

Male and Female

References to the male gender in the Laws of the Game in respect of referees, assistant referees, players and officials are for simplification and apply to both males and females.

Key

Throughout the Laws of the Game the following symbols are used:

* Unless covered by the Special Circumstances listed in Law 8 – The Start and Restart of Play

| A single line indicates new Law changes

|| A double line indicates former International F.A. Board Decisions which are now included in the Laws

WHY WAS **SHEARER** GIVEN SO MUCH ROOM TO **SCORE?**

Flair players need protection if they're to play the kind of football we love to see. That's why referees are a necessary force in football. They enforce the laws of the game. They punish the guilty. But they also protect the innocent. Their presence at every level of the game allows good players to flourish without fear of being clattered every time they collect the ball. Good refereeing encourages good football. And as England prepares for the next World Cup that's exactly what we need. But it's going to take your help. We need referees at every level who will ensure that the next generation of Alan Shearers realise their full potential. For more details phone your local County Football Association, or the FA on 0171 402 7151.

FA REFEREES
WE'RE HERE FOR THE GOOD OF THE GAME

Laws of the Game

Laws of the Game

LAW 1 – The Field of Play

Dimensions

The field of play must be rectangular. The length of the touch line must be greater than the length of the goal line.

Length: minimum 90 m (100 yds)
           maximum 120 m (130 yds)
Width: minimum 45 m (50 yds)
           maximum 90 m (100 yds)

International Matches

Length: minimum 100 m (110 yds)
           maximum 110 m (120 yds)
Width: minimum 64 m (70 yds)
           maximum 75 m (80 yds)

Field Markings

The field of play is marked with lines. These lines belong to the areas of which they are boundaries.

The two longer boundary lines are called touch lines. The two shorter lines are called goal lines.

All lines are not more than 12 cm (5 ins) wide.

The field of play is divided into two halves by a halfway line.

The centre mark is indicated at the midpoint of the halfway line. A circle with a radius of 9.15 m (10 yds) is marked around it.

The Goal Area

A goal area is defined at each end of the field as follows:

Two lines are drawn at right angles to the goal line, 5.5 m (6 yds) from the inside of each goalpost. These lines extend into the field of play for a distance of 5.5 m (6 yds) and are joined by a line drawn parallel with the goal line. The area bounded by these lines and the goal line is the goal area.

The Penalty Area

A penalty area is defined at each end of the field as follows:

Two lines are drawn at right angles to the goal line, 16.5 m (18 yds) from the inside of each goalpost. These lines extend into the field of play for a distance of 16.5 m (18 yds) and are joined by a line drawn parallel with the goal line. The area bounded by these lines and the goal line is the penalty area.

Within each penalty area a penalty mark is made 11 m (12 yds) from the midpoint between the goalposts and equidistant to them. An arc of a circle with a radius of 9.15 m (10 yds) from each penalty mark is drawn outside the penalty area.

Flagposts

A flagpost, not less than 1.5 m (5 ft) high, with a non-pointed top and a flag is placed at each corner.

Flagposts may also be placed at each end of the halfway line, not less than 1m (1 yd) outside the touch line.

The Corner Arc

A quarter circle with a radius of 1 m (1 yd) from each corner flagpost is drawn inside the field of play.

Goals

Goals must be placed on the centre of each goal line.

They consist of two upright posts equidistant from the corner flagposts and joined at the top by a horizontal crossbar.

The distance between the posts is 7.32 m (8 yds) and the distance from the lower edge of the crossbar to the ground is 2.44 m (8ft).

Both goalposts and the crossbar have the same width and depth which do not exceed 12 cm (5 ins). The goal lines are the same width as that of the goalposts and the crossbar. Nets may be attached to the goals and the ground behind the goal, provided that they are properly supported and do not interfere with the goalkeeper.

|| The goalposts and crossbars must be white.

Safety

Goals must be anchored securely to the ground. Portable goals may only be used if they satisfy this requirement.

The Field of Play

Corner Flagpost

Metric Measurements

Imperial Measurements

Decisions of the International F.A. Board

Decision I
If the crossbar becomes displaced or broken, play is stopped until it has been repaired or replaced in position. If a repair is not possible, the match is abandoned. The use of a rope to replace the crossbar is not permitted. If the crossbar can be repaired, the match is restarted with a dropped ball at the place where the ball was located when play was stopped. * (see Key)

Decision 2
Goalposts and crossbars must be made of wood, metal or other approved material. Their shape may be square, rectangular, round or elliptical and they must not be dangerous to players.

Decision 3
No kind of commercial advertising, whether real or virtual, is permitted on the field of play and field equipment (including the goal nets and the areas they enclose) from the time the teams enter the field of play until they have left it at half-time and from the time the teams re-enter the field of play until the end of the match. In particular, no advertising material of any kind may be displayed on goals, nets, flagposts or their flags. No extraneous equipment (cameras, microphones, etc.) may be attached to these items.

Decision 4
The reproduction, whether real or virtual, of representative logos or emblems of FIFA, confederations, national associations, leagues, clubs or other bodies, is forbidden on the field of play and field equipment (including the goal nets and the areas they enclose) during playing time, as described in Decision 3.

Decision 5
A mark may be made off the field of play, 9.15 metres (10 yds) from the corner arc and at right angles to the goal lines to ensure that this distance is observed when a corner kick is being taken.

LAW 2 — The Ball

Qualities and Measurements

The ball is:

- *spherical*

- *made of leather or other suitable material*

- *of a circumference of not more than 70 cm (28 ins) and not less than 68 cm (27 ins)*

- *not more than 450 g (16 oz) in weight and not less than 410 g (14 oz) at the start of the match*

- *of a pressure equal to 0.6 – 1.1 atmosphere (600 – 1100 g/cm2) at sea level (8.5 lbs/sq in 15.6 lbs/sq in)*

Replacement of a Defective Ball

If the ball bursts or becomes defective during the course of a match:

- *the match is stopped*

- *the match is restarted by dropping the replacement ball at the place where the first ball became defective * (see Key)*

If the ball bursts or becomes defective whilst not in play at a kick-off, goal kick, corner kick, free kick, penalty kick or throw-in:

- *the match is restarted accordingly*

The ball may not be changed during the match without the authority of the referee.

Decisions of the International F.A. Board

Decision 1

In competition matches, only footballs which meet the minimum technical requirements stipulated in Law 2 are permitted for use.

In FIFA competition matches, and in competition matches organised under the auspices of the confederations, acceptance of a football for use is conditional upon the football bearing one of the following three designations:

the official 'FIFA APPROVED' logo,

or

the official 'FIFA INSPECTED' logo,

or

the reference 'INTERNATIONAL MATCHBALL STANDARD'

Such a designation on a football indicates that it has been tested officially and found to be in compliance with specific technical requirements, different for each category and additional to the minimum specifications stipulated in Law 2. The list of the additional requirements specific to each of the respective categories must be approved by the International F.A. Board. The institutes conducting the tests are subject to the approval of FIFA.

National association competitions may require the use of balls bearing any one of these three designations.

In all other matches the ball used must satisfy the requirements of Law 2.

Decision 2

In FIFA competition matches and in competition matches organised under the auspices of the confederations and national associations, no kind of commercial advertising on the ball is permitted, except for the emblem of the competition, the competition organiser and the authorised trademark of the manufacturer. The competition regulations may restrict the size and number of such markings.

LAW 3 - The Number of Players

Players

A match is played by two teams, each consisting of not more than eleven players, one of whom is the goalkeeper. A match may not start if either team consists of fewer than seven players.

Official Competitions

Up to a maximum of three substitutes may be used in any match played in an official competition organised under the auspices of FIFA, the confederations or the national associations.

The rules of the competition must state how many substitutes may be nominated, from three up to a maximum of seven.

Other Matches

In other matches, up to five substitutes may be used, provided that:

* *the teams concerned reach agreement on a maximum number*

* *the referee is informed before the match*

If the referee is not informed, or if no agreement is reached before the start of the match, no more than three substitutes are allowed.

All Matches

In all matches the names of the substitutes must be given to the referee prior to the start of the match. Substitutes not so named may not take part in the match.

Substitution Procedure

To replace a player by a substitute, the following conditions must be observed:

- *the referee is informed before any proposed substitution is made*

- *a substitute only enters the field of play after the player being replaced has left and after receiving a signal from the referee*

- *a substitute only enters the field of play at the halfway line and during a stoppage in the match*

- *a substitution is completed when a substitute enters the field of play*

- *from that moment, the substitute becomes a player and the player he has replaced ceases to be a player*

- *a player who has been replaced takes no further part in the match*

- *all substitutes are subject to the authority and jurisdiction of the referee, whether called upon to play or not*

Changing the Goalkeeper

Any of the other players may change places with the goalkeeper, provided that:

- *the referee is informed before the change is made*

- *the change is made during a stoppage in the match*

Infringements/Sanctions

If a substitute enters the field of play without the referee's permission:

- *play is stopped*

- *the substitute is cautioned, shown the yellow card and required to leave the field of play*

- *play is restarted with a dropped ball at the place it was located when play was stopped* (see Key)*

If a player changes places with the goalkeeper without the referee's permission before the change is made:

• *play continues*

• *the players concerned are cautioned and shown the yellow card when the ball is next out of play*

For any other infringements of this Law:

• *the players concerned are cautioned and shown the yellow card*

Restart of Play

If play is stopped by the referee to administer a caution:

• *the match is restarted by an indirect free kick, to be taken by a player of the opposing team from the place where the ball was located when play was stopped * (see Key)*

Players and Substitutes Sent Off

A player who has been sent off before the kick-off may be replaced only by one of the named substitutes.

A named substitute who has been sent off, either before the kick-off or after play has started, may not be replaced.

Decisions of the International F.A. Board

Decision 1

Subject to the overriding conditions of Law 3, the minimum number of players in a team is left to the discretion of national associations. The Board is of the opinion, however, that a match should not continue if there are fewer than seven players in either team.

Decision 2

The coach may convey tactical instructions to the players during the match. He and the other officials must remain within the confines of the technical area, where such an area is provided, and they must behave in a responsible manner.

LAW 4 - The Players' Equipment

Safety

A player must not use equipment or wear anything which is dangerous to himself or another player (including any kind of jewellery).

Basic Equipment

The basic compulsory equipment of a player is:

- *a jersey or shirt*
- *shorts - if thermal undershorts are worn, they are of the same main colour as the shorts*
- *stockings*
- *shinguards*
- *footwear*

Shinguards

- *are covered entirely by the stockings*
- *are made of a suitable material (rubber, plastic, or similar substances)*
- *provide a reasonable degree of protection*

Goalkeepers

- *each goalkeeper wears colours which distinguish him from the other players, the referee and the assistant referees*

Infringements/Sanctions

For any infringement of this Law:

- *play need not be stopped*
- *the player at fault is instructed by the referee to leave the field of play to correct his equipment*

• *the player leaves the field of play when the ball next ceases to be in play, unless he has already corrected his equipment*

• *any player required to leave the field of play to correct his equipment does not re-enter without the referee's permission*

• *the referee checks that the player's equipment is correct before allowing him to re-enter the field of play*

• *the player is only allowed to re-enter the field of play when the ball is out of play*

A player who has been required to leave the field of play because of an infringement of this Law and who enters (or re-enters) the field of play without the referee's permission is cautioned and shown the yellow card.

Restart of Play

If play is stopped by the referee to administer a caution:

• *the match is restarted by an indirect free kick taken by a player of the opposing side, from the place where the ball was located when the referee stopped the match * (see Key)*

LAW 5 – The Referee

The Authority of the Referee

Each match is controlled by a referee who has full authority to enforce the Laws of the Game in connection with the match to which he has been appointed.

Powers and Duties

The Referee:

- *enforces the Laws of the Game*

- *controls the match in co-operation with the assistant referees and, where applicable, with the fourth official*

- *ensures that the ball meets the requirements of Law 2*

- *ensures that the players' equipment meets the requirements of Law 4*

- *acts as timekeeper and keeps a record of the match*

- *stops, suspends or terminates the match, at his discretion, for any infringements of the Laws*

- *stops, suspends or terminates the match because of outside interference of any kind*

- *stops the match if, in his opinion, a player is seriously injured and ensures that he is removed from the field of play*

- *allows play to continue until the ball is out of play if a player is, in his opinion, only slightly injured*

- *ensures that any player bleeding from a wound leaves the field of play. The player may only return on receiving a signal from the referee, who must be satisfied that the bleeding has stopped*

- *allows play to continue when the team against which an offence has been committed will benefit from such an advan-*

tage and penalises the original offence if the anticipated advantage does not ensue at that time

• *punishes the more serious offence when a player commits more than one offence at the same time*

• *takes disciplinary action against players guilty of cautionable and sending-off offences. He is not obliged to take this action immediately but must do so when the ball next goes out of play*

• *takes action against team officials who fail to conduct themselves in a responsible manner and may, at his discretion, expel them from the field of play and its immediate surrounds*

• *acts on the advice of assistant referees regarding incidents which he has not seen*

• *ensures that no unauthorised persons enter the field of play*

• *restarts the match after it has been stopped*

• *provides the appropriate authorities with a match report which includes information on any disciplinary action taken against players, and/or team officials and any other incidents which occurred before, during or after the match*

Decisions of the Referee

The decisions of the referee regarding facts connected with play are final.

The referee may only change a decision on realising that it is incorrect or, at his discretion, on the advice of an assistant referee, provided that he has not restarted play.

Decisions of the International F.A. Board

Decision I

A referee (or where applicable, an assistant referee or fourth official) is not held liable for:

any kind of injury suffered by a player, official or spectator

any damage to property of any kind

any other loss suffered by any individual, club, company, association or other body, which is due or which may be due to any decision which he may take under the terms of the Laws of the Game or in respect of the normal procedures required to hold, play and control a match.

This may include:

• *a decision that the condition of the field of play or its surrounds or that the weather conditions are such as to allow or not to allow a match to take place*

• *a decision to abandon a match for whatever reason*

• *a decision as to the condition of the fixtures or equipment used during a match including the goalposts, crossbar, flagposts and the ball*

• *a decision to stop or not to stop a match due to spectator interference or any problem in the spectator area*

• *a decision to stop or not to stop play to allow an injured player to be removed from the field of play for treatment*

• *a decision to request or insist that an injured player be removed from the field of play for treatment*

• *a decision to allow or not to allow a player to wear certain apparel or equipment*

• *a decision (in so far as this may be his responsibility) to allow or not to allow any persons (including team or stadium officials, security officers, photographers or other media representatives) to be present in the vicinity of the field of play*

• *any other decision which he may take in accordance with the Laws of the Game or in conformity with his duties under the terms of FIFA, confederation, national association or league rules or regulations under which the match is played*

Decision 2

In tournaments or competitions where a fourth official is appointed, his role and duties must be in accordance with the guidelines approved by the International F.A. Board.

LAW 6 – The Assistant Referees

Duties

Two assistant referees are appointed whose duties, subject to the decision of the referee, are to indicate:

- *when the whole of the ball has passed out of the field of play*

- *which side is entitled to a corner kick, goal kick or throw-in*

- *when a player may be penalised for being in an offside position*

- *when a substitution is requested*

- *when misconduct or any other incident has occurred out of the view of the referee*

Assistance

The assistant referees also assist the referee to control the match in accordance with the Laws of the Game.

In the event of undue interference or improper conduct, the referee will relieve an assistant referee of his duties and make a report to the appropriate authorities.

LAW 7 - The Duration of the Match

Periods of Play

The match lasts two equal periods of 45 minutes, unless otherwise mutually agreed between the referee and the two participating teams. Any agreement to alter the periods of play (for example to reduce each half to 40 minutes because of insufficient light) must be made before the start of play and must comply with competition rules.

Half-Time Interval

|| Players are entitled to an interval at half-time.

The half-time interval must not exceed 15 minutes.

Competition rules must state the duration of the half-time interval.

The duration of the half-time interval may be altered only with the consent of the referee.

Allowance for Time Lost

Allowance is made in either period for all time lost through:

- *substitution(s)*
- *assessment of injury to players*
- *removal of injured players from the field of play for treatment*
- *wasting time*
- *any other cause*

The allowance for time lost is at the discretion of the referee.

Penalty Kick

If a penalty kick has to be taken or retaken, the duration of either half is extended until the penalty kick is completed.

Extra Time

Competition rules may provide for two further equal periods to be played. The conditions of Law 8 will apply.

Abandoned Match

An abandoned match is replayed unless the competition rules provide otherwise.

LAW 8 – The Start and Restart of Play

Preliminaries

A coin is tossed and the team which wins the toss decides which goal it will attack in the first half of the match.

The other team takes the kick-off to start the match.

The team which wins the toss takes the kick-off to start the second half of the match.

In the second half of the match the teams change ends and attack the opposite goals.

Kick-off

| A kick-off is a way of starting or restarting play:

- *at the start of the match*
- *after a goal has been scored*
- *at the start of the second half of the match*
- *at the start of each period of extra time, where applicable*

| A goal may be scored directly from the kick-off.

Procedure

- *all players are in their own half of the field*
- *the opponents of the team taking the kick-off are at least 9.15 m (10 yds) from the ball until it is in play*
- *the ball is stationary on the centre mark*
- *the referee gives a signal*
| *• the ball is in play when it is kicked and moves forward*
- *the kicker does not touch the ball a second time until it has touched another player*

After a team scores a goal, the kick-off is taken by the other team.

Infringements/Sanctions

If the kicker touches the ball a second time before it has touched another player:

• *an indirect free kick is awarded to the opposing team to be taken from the place where the infringement occurred* (see Key)*

For any other infringement of the kick-off procedure:

• *the kick-off is retaken*

Dropped Ball

A dropped ball is a way of restarting the match after a temporary stoppage which becomes necessary, while the ball is in play, for any reason not mentioned elsewhere in the Laws of the Game.

Procedure

The referee drops the ball at the place where it was located when play was stopped.* (see Key)

Play restarts when the ball touches the ground.

Infringements/Sanctions

The ball is dropped again:

• *if it is touched by a player before it makes contact with the ground*

• *if the ball leaves the field of play after it makes contact with the ground, without a player touching it*

Special Circumstances

A free kick awarded to the defending team inside its own goal area is taken from any point within the goal area.

An indirect free kick awarded to the attacking team in its opponents' goal area is taken from the goal area line parallel to the goal line at the point nearest to where the infringement occurred.

A dropped ball to restart the match after play has been temporarily stopped inside the goal area takes place on the goal area line parallel to the goal line at the point nearest to where the ball was located when play was stopped.

LAW 9 - The Ball In and Out of Play

Ball Out of Play

The ball is out of play when:

• *it has wholly crossed the goal line or touch line whether on the ground or in the air*

• *play has been stopped by the referee*

Ball In Play

The ball is in play at all other times, including when:

• *it rebounds from a goalpost, crossbar or corner flagpost and remains in the field of play*

• *it rebounds from either the referee or an assistant referee when they are on the field of play*

LAW 10 - The Method of Scoring

Goal Scored

A goal is scored when the whole of the ball passes over the goal line, between the goalposts and under the crossbar, provided that no infringement of the Laws of the Game has been committed previously by the team scoring the goal.

Winning Team

The team scoring the greater number of goals during a match is the winner. If both teams score an equal number of goals, or if no goals are scored, the match is drawn.

Competition Rules

For matches ending in a draw, competition rules may state provisions involving extra time, or other procedures approved by the International F.A. Board to determine the winner of a match.

LAW 11 – Offside

Offside Position

It is not an offence in itself to be in an offside position.

A player is in an offside position if:

• *he is nearer to his opponents' goal line than both the ball and the second last opponent*

A player is not in an offside position if:

• *he is in his own half of the field of play*

or

• *he is level with the second last opponent*

or

• *he is level with the last two opponents*

Offence

A player in an offside position is only penalised if, at the moment the ball touches or is played by one of his team, he is, in the opinion of the referee, involved in active play by:

• *interfering with play*

or

• *interfering with an opponent*

or

• *gaining an advantage by being in that position*

No Offence

There is no offside offence if a player receives the ball directly from:

• *a goal kick*

or

- *a throw-in*

or

- *a corner kick*

Infringements/Sanctions

For any offside offence, the referee awards an indirect free kick to the opposing team to be taken from the place where the infringement occurred.* (see Key)

LAW 12 – Fouls and Misconduct

Fouls and misconduct are penalised as follows:

Direct Free Kick

A direct free kick is awarded to the opposing team if a player commits any of the following six offences in a manner considered by the referee to be careless, reckless or using excessive force:

- *kicks or attempts to kick an opponent*
- *trips or attempts to trip an opponent*
- *jumps at an opponent*
- *charges an opponent*
- *strikes or attempts to strike an opponent*
- *pushes an opponent*

A direct free kick is also awarded to the opposing team if a player commits any of the following four offences:

- *tackles an opponent to gain possession of the ball, making contact with the opponent before touching the ball*
- *holds an opponent*
- *spits at an opponent*
- *handles the ball deliberately (except for the goalkeeper within his own penalty area)*

A direct free kick is taken from where the offence occurred.* (see Key)

Penalty Kick

A penalty kick is awarded if any of the above ten offences is committed by a player inside his own penalty area, irrespective of the position of the ball, provided it is in play.

Indirect Free Kick

An indirect free kick is awarded to the opposing team if a player, in the opinion of the referee, commits any of the following three offences:

- *plays in a dangerous manner*

- *impedes the progress of an opponent*

- *prevents the goalkeeper from releasing the ball from his hands*

An indirect free kick is also awarded to the opposing team if a goalkeeper, inside his own penalty area, commits any of the following five offences:

- *takes more than four steps while controlling the ball with his hands, before releasing it from his possession*

- *touches the ball again with his hands after it has been released from his possession and has not touched any other player*

- *touches the ball with his hands after it has been deliberately kicked to him by a team-mate*

- *touches the ball with his hands after he has received it directly from a throw-in taken by a team-mate*

- *wastes time*

The indirect free kick is taken from where the offence occurred.* (see Key)

Disciplinary Sanctions

Cautionable Offences

A player is cautioned and shown the yellow card if he commits any of the following seven offences:

1. is guilty of unsporting behaviour

2. shows dissent by word or action

3. persistently infringes the Laws of the Game

4. delays the restart of play

5. fails to respect the required distance when play is restarted with a corner kick or free kick

6. enters or re-enters the field of play without the referee's permission

7. deliberately leaves the field of play without the referee's permission

Sending-Off Offences

A player is sent off and shown the red card if he commits any of the following seven offences:

1. is guilty of serious foul play

2. is guilty of violent conduct

3. spits at an opponent or any other person

4. denies an opponent a goal or an obvious goal-scoring opportunity by deliberately handling the ball (this does not apply to a goalkeeper within his own penalty area)

5. denies an obvious goal-scoring opportunity to an opponent moving towards the player's goal by an offence punishable by a free kick or a penalty kick

6. uses offensive, insulting or abusive language

7. receives a second caution in the same match

Decisions of the International F.A. Board

Decision 1
A penalty kick is awarded if, while the ball is in play, the goalkeeper, inside his own penalty area, strikes or attempts to strike an opponent by throwing the ball at him.

Decision 2
A player who commits a cautionable or sending-off offence, either on or off the field of play, whether directed towards an opponent, a team-mate, the referee, an assistant referee or any other person, is disciplined according to the nature of the offence committed.

Decision 3
The goalkeeper is considered to be in control of the ball by touching it with any part of his hand or arms. Possession of the ball includes the goalkeeper deliberately parrying the ball, but does not include the circumstances where, in the opinion of the referee, the ball rebounds accidentally from the goalkeeper, for example after he has made a save.

Decision 4
Subject to the terms of Law 12, a player may pass the ball to his own goalkeeper using his head or chest or knee, etc. If, however, in the opinion of the referee, a player uses a deliberate trick while the ball is in play in order to circumvent the Law, the player is guilty of unsporting behaviour. He is cautioned, shown the yellow card and an indirect free kick is awarded to the opposing team from the place where the infringement occurred. * (see Key)

A player using a deliberate trick to circumvent the Law while he is taking a free kick, is cautioned for unsporting behaviour and shown the yellow card. The free kick is retaken.

In such circumstances, it is irrelevant whether the goalkeeper sub-sequently touches the ball with his hands or not. The offence is commit-ted by the player in attempting to circumvent both the letter and the spirit of Law 12.

LAW 13 - Free Kicks

Types of Free Kicks

Free kicks are either direct or indirect.

For both direct and indirect free kicks, the ball must be stationary when the kick is taken and the kicker does not touch the ball a second time until it has touched another player.

The Direct Free Kick

• *if a direct free kick is kicked directly into the opponents' goal, a goal is awarded*

• *if a direct free kick is kicked directly into the team's own goal, a corner kick is awarded to the opposing team*

The Indirect Free Kick

Signal

The referee indicates an indirect free kick by raising his arm above his head. He maintains his arm in that position until the kick has been taken and the ball has touched another player or goes out of play.

Ball Enters the Goal

A goal can be scored only if the ball subsequently touches another player before it enters the goal.

• *if an indirect free kick is kicked directly into the opponents' goal, a goal kick is awarded*

• *if an indirect free kick is kicked directly into the team's own goal, a corner kick is awarded to the opposing team*

Position of Free Kick

Free Kick Inside the Penalty Area

Direct or indirect free kick to the defending team:

• *all opponents are at least 9.15 m (10 yds) from the ball*

• *all opponents remain outside the penalty area until the ball is in play*

• *the ball is in play when it is kicked directly beyond the penalty area*

• *a free kick awarded in the goal area is taken from any point inside that area*

Indirect free kick to the attacking team:

• *all opponents are at least 9.15 m (10 yds) from the ball until it is in play, unless they are on their own goal line between the goalposts*

| • *the ball is in play when it is kicked and moves*

• *an indirect free kick awarded inside the goal area is taken from that part of the goal area line which runs parallel to the goal line, at the point nearest to where the infringement occurred*

Free Kick Outside the Penalty Area

• *all opponents are at least 9.15 m (10 yds) from the ball until it is in play*

| • *the ball is in play when it is kicked and moves*

• *the free kick is taken from the place where the infringement occurred*

Infringements/Sanctions

If, when a free kick is taken, an opponent is closer to the ball than the required distance:

| • *the kick is retaken*

If, when a free kick is taken by the defending team from inside its own penalty area, the ball is not kicked directly into play:

• *the kick is retaken*

Free kick taken by a player other than the goalkeeper

If, after the ball is in play, the kicker touches the ball a second time (except with his hands) before it has touched another player:

• *an indirect free kick is awarded to the opposing team, the kick to be taken from the place where the infringement occurred* (see Key)*

If, after the ball is in play, the kicker deliberately handles the ball before it has touched another player:

• *a direct free kick is awarded to the opposing team, the kick to be taken from the place where the infringement occurred* (see Key)*

• *a penalty kick is awarded if the infringement occurred inside the kicker's penalty area*

Free Kick taken by the goalkeeper

If, after the ball is in play, the goalkeeper touches the ball a second time (except with his hands), before it has touched another player:

• *an indirect free kick is awarded to the opposing team, the kick to be taken from the place where the infringement occurred* (see Key)*

If, after the ball is in play, the goalkeeper deliberately handles the ball before it has touched another player:

• *a direct free kick is awarded to the opposing team if the infringement occurred outside the goalkeeper's penalty area, the kick to be taken from the place where the infringement occurred* (see Key)*

• *an indirect free kick is awarded to the opposing team if the infringement occurred inside the goalkeeper's penalty area, the kick to be taken from the place where the infringement occurred * (see Key)*

LAW 14 – The Penalty Kick

A penalty kick is awarded against a team which commits one of the ten offences for which a direct free kick is awarded, inside its own penalty area and while the ball is in play.

A goal may be scored directly from a penalty kick.

Additional time is allowed for a penalty kick to be taken at the end of each half or at the end of periods of extra time.

Position of the Ball and the Players

The ball:

- *is placed on the penalty mark*

The player taking the penalty kick:

- *is properly identified*

The defending goalkeeper:

- *remains on his goal line, facing the kicker, between the goalposts until the ball has been kicked*

The players other than the kicker are located:

- *inside the field of play*
- *outside the penalty area*
- *behind the penalty mark*
- *at least 9.15 m (10 yds) from the penalty mark*

The Referee

- *does not signal for a penalty kick to be taken until the players have taken up position in accordance with the Law*
- *decides when a penalty kick has been completed*

Procedure

• *the player taking the penalty kicks the ball forward*

• *he does not play the ball a second time until it has touched another player*

| • *the ball is in play when it is kicked and moves forward*

When a penalty kick is taken during the normal course of play, or time has been extended at half-time or full time to allow a penalty kick to be taken or retaken, a goal is awarded if, before passing between the goalposts and under the crossbar:

• *the ball touches either or both of the goalposts and/or the crossbar, and/or the goalkeeper*

Infringements/Sanctions

If the referee gives the signal for a penalty kick to be taken and, before the ball is in play, one of the following situations occurs:

The player taking the penalty kick infringes the Laws of the Game:

• *the referee allows the kick to proceed*

• *if the ball enters the goal, the kick is retaken*

• *if the ball does not enter the goal, the kick is not retaken*

The goalkeeper infringes the Laws of the Game:

• *the referee allows the kick to proceed*

• *if the ball enters the goal, a goal is awarded*

• *if the ball does not enter the goal, the kick is retaken*

A team-mate of the player taking the kick enters the penalty area or moves in front of or within 9.5 m (10 yds) of the penalty mark:

| • *the referee allows the kick to proceed*

| • *if the ball enters the goal, the kick is retaken*

| • *if the ball does not enter the goal, the kick is not retaken*

A team-mate of the goalkeeper enters the penalty area or moves in front of or within 9.15 m (10 yds) of the penalty mark:

| • *the referee allows the kick to proceed*

| • *if the ball enters the goal, a goal is awarded*

| • *if the ball does not enter the goal, the kick is retaken*

A player of both the defending team and the attacking team infringe the Laws of the Game:

| • *the kick is retaken*

If, after the penalty kick has been taken:

The kicker touches the ball a second time (except with his hands) before it has touched another player:

• *an indirect free kick is awarded to the opposing team, the kick to be taken from the place where the infringement occurred* (see Key)*

The kicker deliberately handles the ball before it has touched another player:

• *a direct free kick is awarded to the opposing team, the kick to be taken from the place where the infringement occurred* (see Key)*

The ball is touched by an outside agent as it moves forward:

• *the kick is retaken*

The ball rebounds into the field of play from the goalkeeper, the crossbar or the goalposts, and is then touched by an outside agent:

• *the referee stops play*

• *play is restarted with a dropped ball at the place where it touched the outside agent* (see Key)*

LAW 15 – The Throw-In

A throw-in is a method of restarting play.

A goal cannot be scored directly from a throw-in.

A throw-in is awarded:

• *when the whole of the ball passes over the touch line, either on the ground or in the air*

• *from the point where it crossed the touch line*

• *to the opponents of the player who last touched the ball*

Procedure

At the moment of delivering the ball, the thrower:

• *faces the field of play*

• *has part of each foot either on the touch line or on the ground outside the touch line*

• *uses both hands*

• *delivers the ball from behind and over his head*

The thrower may not touch the ball again until it has touched another player.

The ball is in play immediately it enters the field of play.

Infringements/Sanctions

Throw-in taken by a player other than the goalkeeper

If, after the ball is in play, the thrower touches the ball a second time (except with his hands) before it has touched another player:

• *an indirect free kick is awarded to the opposing team, the kick to be taken from the place where the infringement occurred* (see Key)*

If, after the ball is in play, the thrower deliberately handles the ball before it has touched another player:

• *a direct free kick is awarded to the opposing team, the kick to be taken from the place where the infringement occurred* (see Key)*

• *a penalty kick is awarded if the infringement occurred inside the thrower's penalty area*

Throw-in taken by the goalkeeper

If, after the ball is in play, the goalkeeper touches the ball a second time (except with his hands), before it has touched another player:

• *an indirect free kick is awarded to the opposing team, the kick to be taken from the place where the infringement occurred* (see Key)*

If, after the ball is in play, the goalkeeper deliberately handles the ball before it has touched another player:

• *a direct free kick is awarded to the opposing team if the infringement occurred outside the goalkeeper's penalty area, the kick to be taken from the place where the infringement occurred* (see Key)*

• *an indirect free kick is awarded to the opposing team if the infringement occurred inside the goalkeeper's penalty area, the kick to be taken from the place where the infringement occurred* (see Key)*

If an opponent unfairly distracts or impedes the thrower:

- *he is cautioned for unsporting behaviour and shown the yellow card*

For any other infringement of this Law:

- *the throw-in is taken by a player of the opposing team*

LAW 16 – The Goal Kick

A goal kick is a method of restarting play.

A goal may be scored directly from a goal kick, but only against the opposing team.

A goal kick is awarded when:

• *the whole of the ball, having last touched a player of the attacking team, passes over the goal line, either on the ground or in the air, and a goal is not scored in accordance with Law 10*

Procedure

• *the ball is kicked from any point within the goal area by a player of the defending team*

• *opponents remain outside the penalty area until the ball is in play*

• *the kicker does not play the ball a second time until it has touched another player*

• *the ball is in play when it is kicked directly beyond the penalty area*

Infringements/Sanctions

If the ball is not kicked directly into play beyond the penalty area:

• *the kick is retaken*

Goal kick taken by a player other than the goalkeeper

If, after the ball is in play, the kicker touches the ball a second time (except with his hands) before it has touched another player:

• *an indirect free kick is awarded to the opposing team, the kick to be taken from the place where the infringement occurred* * *(see Key)*

If, after the ball is in play, the kicker deliberately handles the ball before it has touched another player:

• *a direct free kick is awarded to the opposing team, the kick to be taken from the place where the infringement occurred* (see Key)*

• *a penalty kick is awarded if the infringement occurred inside the kicker's penalty area*

Goal kick taken by the goalkeeper

If, after the ball is in play, the goalkeeper touches the ball a second time (except with his hands) before it has touched another player:

• *an indirect free kick is awarded to the opposing team, the kick to be taken from the place where the infringement occurred* (see Key)*

If, after the ball is in play, the goalkeeper deliberately handles the ball before it has touched another player:

• *a direct free kick is awarded to the opposing team if the infringement occurred outside the goalkeeper's penalty area, the kick to be taken from the place where the infringement occurred* (see Key)*

• *an indirect free kick is awarded to the opposing team if the infringement occurred inside the goalkeeper's penalty area, the kick to be taken from the place where the infringement occurred* (see Key)*

For any other infringement of this Law:

• *the kick is retaken*

A corner kick is a method of restarting play.

A goal may be scored directly from a corner kick, but only against the opposing team.

A corner kick is awarded when:

- *the whole of the ball, having last touched a player of the defending team, passes over the goal line, either on the ground or in the air, and a goal is not scored in accordance with Law 10*

Procedure

- *the ball is placed inside the corner arc at the nearest corner flagpost*

- *the corner flagpost is not moved*

- *opponents remain at least 9.15 m (10 yds) from the ball until it is in play*

- *the ball is kicked by a player of the attacking team*

- *the ball is in play when it is kicked and moves*

- *the kicker does not play the ball a second time until it has touched another player*

Infringements/Sanctions

A corner kick taken by a player other than the goalkeeper

If, after the ball is in play, the kicker touches the ball a second time (except with his hands), before it has touched another player:

- *an indirect free kick is awarded to the opposing team, the kick to be taken from the place where the infringement occurred* * (see Key)*

Play On – Advantage. Where the referee sees an offence but uses the Advantage, he shall indicate that play shall continue

Indirect Free-kick. This signal shall be maintained until the kick has been taken and retained until the ball has been played or touched by another player or goes out of play

Direct Free-kick. The hand and arm clearly indicate the direction

Penalty-kick. The referee clearly indicates the penalty-mark, but there is no need to run towards it

Goal-kick

Corner-kick

Caution or Expulsion. With the card system in operation, the card shall be shown in the manner illustrated. The player's identity *must* be recorded at the time

Off-side. Flag held upright to indicate Off-side

Off-side. When the referee stops play, assistant referee indicates position of far side of the field

Off-side. Position on near side of the field

Off-side. Position near the centre of the field

Throw-in

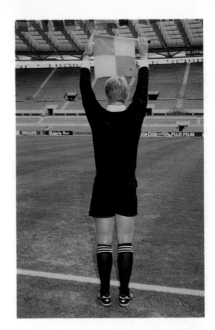

Back view of the assistant referee signalling to the referee for a substitution to be made

Front view of the assistant referee signalling to the referee when a substitute is waiting at the touch-line

Corner-kick. The assistant referee may first need to signal that the ball has gone out of play if there is any doubt. He should also look at the referee in case he has already made his own decision which may be different from the assistant referee's

Goal-kick

If, after the ball is in play, the kicker deliberately handles the ball before it has touched another player:

• *a direct free kick is awarded to the opposing team, the kick to be taken from the place where the infringement occurred * (see Key)*

• *a penalty kick is awarded if the infringement occurred inside the kicker's penalty area*

Corner kick taken by the goalkeeper

If, after the ball is in play, the goalkeeper touches the ball a second time (except with his hands) before it has touched another player:

• *an indirect free kick is awarded to the opposing team, the kick to be taken from the place where the infringement occurred* (see Key)*

If, after the ball is in play, the goalkeeper deliberately handles the ball before it has touched another player:

• *a direct free kick is awarded to the opposing team if the infringement occurred outside the goalkeeper's penalty area, the kick to be taken from the place where the infringement occurred * (see Key)*

• *an indirect free kick is awarded to the opposing team if the infringement occurred inside the goalkeeper's penalty area, the kick to be taken from the place where the infringement occurred * (see Key)*

For any other infringement:

• *the kick is retaken*

Kicks from the Penalty Mark

Procedures and Check-list for Referees

The International Board at its Meeting on 27th June 1970 accepted a proposal by The Fédération Internationale de Football Association that the practice of drawing lots to determine which of two teams in a drawn match should proceed to a later stage of a Knock-Out Competition or receive the trophy (if any) be discontinued and be replaced by the taking of kicks from the penalty mark which shall not be considered part of the match, subject to the following conditions:–

1 The Referee shall choose the goal at which all of the kicks shall be taken.

2 He shall toss a coin, and the team whose captain wins the toss shall take the first kick.

3 The Referee will record the names of the players who have taken the kicks from the penalty mark, in order to ensure that the provisions of paragraph 7, below, are adhered to.

4 (a) Subject to the terms of the following paragraphs (c) and (d) both teams shall take five kicks.
  (b) The kicks shall be taken alternately.
  (c) If, before both teams have taken five kicks, one has scored more goals than the other could, even if it were to complete its five kicks, the taking of kicks shall cease.
  (d) If, after both teams have taken five kicks, both have scored the same number of goals, or have not scored any goals, the taking of kicks shall continue in the same order, until such time as both have taken an equal number of kicks (not necessarily five more kicks) and one has scored a goal more than the other.

5   The team which scores the greater number of goals, whether the number of kicks taken is in accordance with the terms of the foregoing paragraph 4(*a*), 4(*c*) or 4(*d*) shall qualify for the next round of the competition, or shall be declared winner of the competition, as the case may be.

6   (*a*) With the exception referred to in the following paragraph (*b*) only the players who are on the field of play at the end of the match, which shall mean at the end of extra time in so far as a match in which extra time is authorized is concerned, and any who, having left the field temporarily, with or without the Referee's permission, are not on the field of play at that time, shall take part in the taking of the kicks.

(*b*) Provided that his team has not already made use of the maximum number of substitutes permitted by the rules of the competition under which the match was played, a goalkeeper who sustains an injury during the taking of the kicks, and who, because of the injury, is unable to continue as goalkeeper may be replaced by a substitute.

7   Each kick shall be taken by a different player, and not until all eligible players of any team, including the goalkeeper or the named substitute by whom he was replaced in terms of paragraph **6** as the case may be, have each taken a kick may a player of the same team take a second kick.

8   Subject to the terms of paragraph **6** any player who is eligible may change places with his goalkeeper at any time during the taking of the kicks.

9   (*a*) Other than the player taking a kick from the penalty mark, and the two goalkeepers, all players shall remain within the centre circle whilst the taking of kicks is in progress.

(*b*) The goalkeeper who is a colleague of the kicker, shall take up position within the field of play, outside the penalty area at which the kicks are being taken, behind the line which runs parallel with the goal-line, and at least 10 yards from the penalty mark.

10 Unless stated to the contrary in the foregoing paragraphs 1 to **9**, the Laws of the Game, and the International Board Decisions relating thereto, shall, in so far as they can, apply at the taking of the kicks.

N.B. In the event of light failing before the end of the taking of kicks from the penalty mark, the result shall be decided by the toss of a coin or the drawing of lots.

Check-list for Referees

1   Decide at which end the kicks will be taken. This can be an important decision if the supporters of one team are behind one goal and those of the other team are at the opposite goal.

2   The team which wins the toss must take the first kick.

3   Before the kicks begin, ensure that all club officials, etc., have left the field and that only the players are left.

4   Make sure all players, apart from the kicker and the two goalkeepers, are inside the centre circle.

5   Make sure the goalkeeper of the kicker's team stands outside the penalty area.

6   The Laws of the Game, particularly **Law XIV** 'The Penalty-Kick', apply except where modified by the instructions for the taking of kicks from the penalty mark. Be particularly vigilant therefore for instances of gamesmanship or for infringements by the goalkeeper, e.g. moving before the ball is kicked.

7   Keep a careful record of the kicks taken.

8   Where you have the assistance of Assistant Referees some of those duties may be taken by them, e.g. an Assistant Referee at the centre circle would organize players coming to take the kick while the other Assistant Referee would assist by indicating whether or not the ball has crossed the goal-line.

9   It is very important that the referee organizes the taking of kicks from the penalty mark correctly. Make sure you fully understand the instructions.

10 The taking of kicks from the penalty mark never forms part of an actual match. It is only a method of deciding a winner.

11 If, at the taking of kicks from the penalty mark, the light fails badly and the kicks therefore cannot be completed, the result shall be decided by the tossing of a coin or the drawing of lots.

12 An injured player may be excused from the taking of kicks from the penalty mark.

13 It is the responsibility of each team to select the players who will take the kicks from the penalty mark. The Referee's only duty is to ensure that they are taken correctly.

14 When all the players in a team have taken a kick from the penalty mark, it is not necessary that they follow the same order in taking their second kick as they had for the first series of kicks.

15 If a player who has already been cautioned commits a second cautionable offence at the taking of kicks from the penalty mark, he shall be sent off.

16 If the lights fail at a stadium after extra time but before the taking of kicks from the penalty mark, and if they cannot be repaired in a reasonable time, the referee shall decide the match by tossing a coin or drawing lots.

17 A substitute who has not taken part in the match, including extra time where it is played, may not take part in kicks from the penalty mark, except to replace an injured goalkeeper.

18 After each team has taken 10 kicks from the penalty mark, a team which has had a player sent off may use a player who has already taken a kick for the 11th kick.

19 If at the end of the match some players leave the field of play and fail to return for the taking of kicks from the penalty mark, and are not injured, the Referee will not allow the kicks to be taken and will report the matter to the responsible authorities.

20 If, at the taking of kicks from the penalty mark, or when extended time is being allowed for a penalty-kick to be taken in normal playing time, the ball strikes the goal-post or cross-bar, strikes the goalkeeper and enters the goal, a goal shall be awarded.

The Technical Area

The technical area described in Law 3, International F.A. Board Decision no. 2, relates particularly to matches played in stadia with a designated seated area for technical staff and substitutes.

Technical areas may vary between stadia, for example in size or location, and the following notes are issued for general guidance.

• *The technical area extends 1 m (1 yd) on either side of the designated seated area and extends forward up to a distance of 1 m (1 yd) from the touch line.*

• *It is recommended that markings are used to define this area.*

• *The number of persons permitted to occupy the technical area is defined by the competition rules.*

• *The occupants of the technical area are identified before the beginning of the match in accordance with the competition rules.*

• *Only one person at a time is authorised to convey tactical instructions and he must return to his position immediately after giving these instructions.*

• *The coach and other officials must remain within the confines of the technical area except in special circumstances, for example, a physiotherapist or doctor entering the field of play, with the referee's permission, to assess an injured player.*

* *The coach and other occupants of the technical area must behave in a responsible manner.*

The Fourth Official

- *The fourth official may be appointed under the competition rules and officiates if any of the three match officials is unable to continue.*

- *Prior to the start of the competition, the organiser states clearly whether, if the referee is unable to continue, the fourth official takes over as the match referee or whether the senior assistant referee takes over as referee with the fourth official becoming an assistant referee.*

- *The fourth official assists with any administrative duties before, during and after the match, as required by the referee.*

- *He is responsible for assisting with substitution procedures during the match.*

• *He supervises the replacement footballs, where required. If the match ball has to be replaced during a match, he provides another ball, on the instruction of the referee, thus keeping the delay to a minimum.*

• *He has the authority to check the equipment of substitutes before they enter the field of play. If their equipment does not comply with the Laws of the Game, he informs the assistant referee, who then informs the referee.*

• *The fourth official assists the referee at all times.*

• *After the match, the fourth official must submit a report to the appropriate authorities on any misconduct or other incident which has occurred out of the view of the referee and the assistant referees. The fourth official must advise the referee and his assistants of any report being made.*

Signals by the Referee and Assistant Referees

The signals used in this Memorandum have been approved by the International F.A. Board for use by registered Referees of affiliated National Associations. The signals are simple, universally in use and well understood.

1   While it is not the duty of the Referee to explain or mime any offence that has caused him to give a particular decision, there are times when a **simple gesture** or word of guidance can aid communication and assist toward greater understanding, and gaining more respect, to the mutual benefit of both Referee and players. Improving communication should be encouraged, but the **exaggerated miming** of offences can be undignified and confusing and **should not be used**.

2   An indication by the Referee of the point where a throw-in should be taken may well help a player from taking a throw-in improperly. A call of **'Play On: Advantage'** *confirms to the player that the Referee has not missed a foul*, but has chosen to apply advantage. Even an indication that the ball was minutely deflected by touching another player on its path across a touchline might be helpful in generating a greater understanding between Referee and players. A better understanding will lead to more harmonious relationships.

3   **All signals given by the Referee should be simple, clear and instinctive.** They should be designed to control the game efficiently and to ensure continuous play as far as is possible; they are intended essentially to indicate what the next action in the game should be, not principally to justify that action.

4   An arm pointing to indicate a corner-kick, goal-kick or foul, and the direction in which the kick is to be taken, will normally be sufficient. **The raised arm to indicate that a free-kick is indirect** is clearly understood, but if a player queries politely

whether the award is a direct free-kick or an indirect free-kick, a helpful word from the Referee, in addition to the regular signal, will lead to a better understanding in future.

5 The duties of the Referee and Assistant Referees are set out briefly but clearly in the Laws of the Game, **Laws 5** and **6**.

6 There is a further exposition of co-operation between the Referee and Assistant Referees in the Memorandum explaining the universally adopted system of 'Diagonal Control'.

7 The proper use of the whistle, voice and hand signals by the Referee and the flags by the Assistant Referees should all assist understanding through clear communication.

Co-operation between Assistant Referees and Referee

8 When play has been stopped the Assistant Referee should assist the Referee by signalling in the following manner for the following incidents:

1 **Off-Side.** The Assistant Referee should lower his flag a full arm's length to the positions illustrated, and point across the field of play to indicate the spot from which the kick should be taken. The only exception would be where the Referee has decided to position himself to judge off-side when play develops from a corner-kick, penalty-kick or free-kick close to goal.

2 **Throw-In.** When the ball goes out of play over the touch-line on his side of the field, the Assistant Referee should indicate the direction of the throw. He should also signal if the thrower's feet, at the moment of release of the ball, are incorrectly placed.

3 **Corner- and Goal-Kicks.** When the whole of the ball goes out of play over the goal-line the Assistant Referee should indicate whether a corner-kick or a goal-kick should be given.

4 **Goal.** When the Referee indicates that a goal is scored the Assistant Referee should return quickly to his position towards the half-way line.

Law XII. If the Assistant Referee senses that the Referee has not seen an infringement he should raise his flag high. If the Referee stops play the Assistant Referee should indicate the direction of the free-kick (direct or indirect), otherwise he shall lower his flag.

5 Substitution. When a substitution is to be made the Assistant Referee nearest the point of substitution shall attract the attention of the Referee by raising his flag as shown in the illustration included in the colour section.

Memorandum on co-operation between Referees and Assistant Referees

Co-operation between Referee and Assistant Referees – Law 6

In the Laws of the Game set out in the foregoing pages there are no instructions as to the relative positioning of Referee and Assistant Referees during a game. There are, however, instructions in **Laws 5** and **6** with regard to powers and duties of Referees and Assistant Referees which rightly interpreted would mean co-operation. **Law 6** stipulates that two Assistant Referees shall be appointed, whose duty (subject to the decision of the Referee) shall be:

(a) To indicate WHEN the ball is out of play.
(b) To indicate when the ball has crossed the goal-line and whether a corner-kick or a goal-kick is to be awarded.
(c) To indicate which side is entitled to the throw-in.
(d) To assist the Referee in carrying out the game in accordance with the Laws.

The assistance referred to in (d) is:
(1) Signalling when the WHOLE of the ball is out of play.
(2) Indicating WHICH side is entitled to the corner-kick, the goal-kick, or the throw-in.
(3) Calling the attention of the Referee to rough play or ungentlemanly conduct.
(4) Giving an opinion on any point on which the Referee may consult him.
(5) **Substitution.** When a substitution is to be made, the Assistant Referee nearest to the point of substitution shall attract the attention of the Referee by raising his flag as shown in the illustration included in the colour section.

Neutral Assistant Referees

The assistance referred to above is best given by NEUTRAL ASSIST-ANT REFEREES. A limitation is placed upon CLUB LINESMEN because points (2), (3) and (4) are not usually referred to those who are not neutral. It is appreciated that there must be a different attitude adopted by the Referee in the case of Assistant Referees, because in effect there are THREE officials supervising the play; the REFEREE remains as principal official, but the Assistant Referees are there to assist him to control the game in a proper manner.

Club Linesmen

To get the most effective co-operation from CLUB LINESMEN the following procedure should be adopted:

(1) BOTH Club Linesmen should report to the Referee BEFORE the start of the match, and receive his instructions, and be informed that no matter what may be their personal opinion the decision of the Referee is final, and must not be questioned.

(2) The work allotted to them as Club Linesmen is to signal WHEN the ball is ENTIRELY over the touch-line, and to indicate WHICH side is entitled to the throw-in, subject always to the decisions of the Referee.

Keeping in mind their distinctive duties outlined above Referees should decide beforehand exactly WHAT they want their Club Linesmen to do, and should be able to tell them distinctly how they can best help him. It is essential that there should be some conference between the three officials BEFORE any match. As the chief of this trio, the Referee must be able to indicate clearly to his assistants how they may best help him. His instructions must be specific, in order to avoid confusion. On their side, the ASSISTANT REFEREES must fully appreciate the Referee's prior authority, and accept his rulings without question, should there be any difference of opinion amongst them. Their relationship to him MUST be one of assistance and neither undue intervention nor opposition.

The Referee will operate the diagonal system of control when his Assistant Referees are neutral. When they are Club Linesmen he shall inform them which method he intends to operate. He will co-operate with his Assistant Referees on the following matters and indicate to them:–

(a) The time by his watch.

(b) The side of the field which each Assistant Referee will take in each half of the match.

(c) Their duties prior to the commencement of the game, such as the examination of the appurtenances of the game.

(d) Which shall be the senior Assistant Referee in case of need.

(e) The position to be taken for corner-kicks.

(f) The sign that he has noticed his Assistant Referee, but has overruled the indication therefrom.

(g) Which action in the throw-in shall be in the province of the Assistant Referee, and which that of the Referee, e.g., many Referees ask their Assistant Referees to watch for foot faults whilst they look for the hand faults.

Referees should not necessarily keep to one diagonal of the field of play. If the state of the ground, wind, sun or other conditions demand a change to the opposite diagonal, a Referee should indicate to his Assistant Referees his intention to make such a change-over, and the Assistant Referees will at once take over the other half of their particular lines. One advantage of such a change of diagonal is that the surface of the ground, next to the touch-line, will be less severely worn because the whole length of the field will be utilized.

Other co-operative matters may be added, but it is important that each of these should be known to the three officials.

The following diagrams illustrate the diagonal system of control, and if studied and practised will lead to uniform methods of control.

The Diagonal System of Control

Diagram One

The imaginary diagonal used by the Referee is the line **A–B**; the cross diagonal used by the Assistant Referee is adjusted to the position of the Referee.

If the Referee is near **A**, Assistant Referee **AR2** will be at a point between **M** and **K**; when the Referee is at **B**, Assistant Referee **AR1** will be between **E** and **F**. This gives TWO Officials control of the respective '*danger zones*', one at each side of the field.

Assistant Referee AR1 adopts the REDS as his side; **Assistant Referee AR2** adopts the BLUES. As RED forwards move towards the BLUE goal, Assistant Referee **AR1** keeps up with their foremost man, so in actual practice he will rarely get into RED's half of the field. Similarly Assistant Referee **AR2** keeps up with the foremost BLUE's player, and will rarely get into BLUE's half.

At **corner-kicks** or **penalty-kicks** the Assistant Referee in that half where the corner-kick or penalty-kick occurs positions himself at **N** and the Referee takes positions illustrated in **Diagram 4**: Corner-kick and **Diagram 9**: Penalty-kick.

The Diagonal System **fails** if Assistant Referee **AR2** gets between **G** and **H** when the Referee is at **B**; or when Assistant Referee **AR1** is near **C** or **D** when the referee is at **A**. Then there are TWO Officials at the same place – **this should be avoided.**

(N.B. – Some Referees prefer to use the opposite diagonal, from F to M, in which case the Assistant Referees should adjust their positions accordingly.)

DIAGRAM I

DIAGRAM 2

START OF GAME

Position of Referee at Kick-off – R.
Position of Assistant Referees – AR1 and AR2.
Players – ○ and ●.
Diagonal followed by Referee – A —— B.
Referee moves to diagonal along line ← ——→ according to direction of attack.
Ball – ⊗.

DIAGRAM 3

DEVELOPMENT OF ATTACK

(From Diagram 2)

Ball moves out to left wing, Referee (R) slightly off diagonal to be near play.
Assistant Referee (AR2) level with spearhead of attack.
Two officials, therefore, up with play.
Assistant Referee (AR1) in position for clearance and possible counter attack.

DIAGRAM 4

CORNER-KICK

Position of officials the same no matter at which corner-area the kick is taken. Referee (R) alongside goal-post, or at position shown.

Concerning the position of the Assistant Referee No. 2, in accordance with the instructions from the Referee the Assistant Referee No. 2 (AR2) shall be near the corner flag or on the goal-line near the corner flag, to observe whether the ball is properly played, whether the opposing players are at proper distance (10 yards), whether the ball is behind the goal-line, or whether incidents have happened possibly hidden from the Referee.

Assistant Referee (AR1) in position for clearance and possible counter attack.

DIAGRAM 5

THE COUNTER-ATTACK

(Following Diagram 4)

Referee (R) sprints to regain correct position on diagonal along
path — — — →
(Note: The Referee who is physically fit is able to do this easily.)
Assistant Referee (AR2) hurries back to his correct position on the touch-
line.
Assistant Referee (AR1) level with attack and in position to see infringements
and indicate decisions until Referee regains his position.

DIAGRAM 6

GOAL-KICK

Referee (R) in midfield adjacent to central point of diagonal.

Assistant Referee (AR1) exercising watch over goal-kick.

Assistant Referee (AR2) in position pending a possible attack by side taking goal-kick.

DIAGRAM 7

FREE-KICK IN MIDFIELD

Players lined up for kick ● and ○. Referee (R) and Assistant Referee (AR2) in respective diagonal positions, level with players and able to judge accurately any questions of off-side or foul play. Assistant Referee (AR1) sees that kick is taken from correct position and also is in position for possible counter attack.

DIAGRAM 8

FREE-KICK NEAR GOAL

(Just outside penalty-area)

Players ● and ○ line up for free-kick.
Referee (R) takes up his position just off his diagonal so that he is placed accurately to judge off-side. Assistant Referee (AR2) is more advanced but can watch for off-side and fouls and also is in a good position to act as goal judge in the event of a direct shot being taken.

DIAGRAM 9

PENALTY-KICK

Players ● and ○ with the exception of the goalkeeper and kicker are shown outside the penalty area and at least 10 yards from the ball – goalkeeper on goal-line.

Referee (R) is in position to see that kick is properly taken and that no encroachment takes place.

Assistant Referee (AR2) watches goalkeeper to see that he does not advance illegally and also acts as goal judge.

Assistant Referee (AR1) is in position should the goalkeeper save a goal and start a counter attack.

DIAGRAM 10 (A)

THROW-IN

Ball out of play and Assistant Referee (AR2) is in position to indicate position of throw and to which side.

Referee (R) crosses from diagonal to centre of field, in the same manner as a defence covering a throw-in.

Assistant Referee (AR1) watches his forward line against the possible counter attack.

DIAGRAM 10 (B)

THROW-IN

Assistant Referee (AR1) is away from the throw-in but should be able to judge feet and probably to indicate which side is entitled to throw. He also maintains his position in the event of a clearance.

Referee (R) can judge other throw-in infringements and veers slightly from his diagonal towards touch-line.

Assistant Referee (AR2) is in position to see any infringement occurring before Referee can turn to follow play.

Diagrams illustrating points in connection with OFF-SIDE

NOTE: The players marked ⊗ are attacking the goal and those marked ○ are defending.

Direction of movement of the ball ———→

Direction of movement of player ———→

DIAGRAM 1 – OFF-SIDE

Pass to a Team Mate

A passes the ball to **B**.

B is off-side because he is in front of **A** and is nearer to his opponents' goal-line than at least two opponents when the ball was passed by **A**.

DIAGRAM 2 – NOT OFF-SIDE

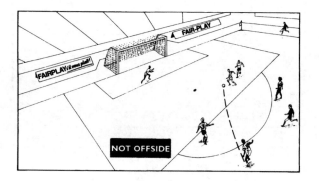

Pass to a Team Mate (continued)

A plays the ball forward to **B** who is level with the second last defender.

B is not off-side since, at the moment the ball was played by **A**, he was not nearer to his opponents' goal-line than at least two of his opponents.

DIAGRAM 3 – NOT OFF-SIDE

Pass to a Team Mate

A plays the ball forward to B who is level with the second last defender.

B is not off-side since, at the moment the ball was played by A, he was not nearer to his opponents' goal-line than at least two of his opponents.

Player C, lying injured outside the penalty area, is in an off-side position but would not be penalised since he is not involved in active play.

DIAGRAM 4 – NOT OFF-SIDE

Pass to a Team Mate (continued)

A plays the ball to B who is level with the last two opponents.

B is not off-side since at the moment the ball was played by A, he was not nearer his opponents' goal-line than at least two of his opponents.

DIAGRAM 5 – OFF-SIDE

Pass to a Team Mate (continued)

A crosses the ball forward from outside the penalty area.

B runs from Position 1 and collects the ball as it lands at Position 2.

B is off-side since, at the moment the ball was played by **A**, he was nearer to his opponents' goal-line than at least two of his opponents and gained an advantage by being in active play.

DIAGRAM 6 – NOT OFF-SIDE

Pass to a Team Mate (continued)

A passes the ball to B who runs from Position 1 to Position 2 to play it.

B is not off-side because at the moment the ball was played by A, he was not in an off-side position since he was not in front of the ball and was not nearer to his opponents' goal-line than at least two of his opponents.

DIAGRAM 7 – OFF-SIDE

Inter-passing with a Team Mate

A plays the ball to **B** from Position 1 and runs forward to receive the return pass.

B plays the ball to **A** who is now in Position 2.

A is off-side since at the moment the ball was played forward to him by **B**, he was nearer his opponents' goal-line than at least two of his opponents and gained an advantage by being in active play.

DIAGRAM 8 – OFF-SIDE

Interfering with an Opponent

A shoots for goal and the ball enters the net.

B is standing in front of the goalkeeper.

The goal would not be allowed since B, who is in an off-side position, is involved in active play and is interfering with an opponent.

DIAGRAM 9 – NOT OFF-SIDE

Shot at Goal

A shoots for goal and scores.

Although **B** is in an off-side position, he is not involved in active play and the goal would be allowed.

DIAGRAM 10 – OFF-SIDE

Ball Rebounding from Goal Posts or Crossbar

A shoots for goal and the ball rebounds from the post to B who kicks the ball into goal.

The goal would be disallowed since B, who was in an off-side position when the ball was last played by A, was in active play and gained an advantage by being in that position.

DIAGRAM 11 – NOT OFF-SIDE

Not Interfering with an Opponent

A shoots for goal and scores.

Although B is lying injured in an off-side position, he is not involved in active play.

The goal would be allowed.

DIAGRAM 12 – OFF-SIDE

Interfering with an Opponent

A shoots for goal and the ball enters the net.

B, who is lying injured in the goal area and in the path of the ball, would be penalised for off-side. By his presence, however accidental, he is involved in the active play and is interfering with an opponent.

DIAGRAM 13 – OFF-SIDE

Shot Rebounds from Goalkeeper

A shoots the ball at goal and the ball rebounds from the goalkeeper to player **B**.

The goal is disallowed since **B**, who was in an off-side position when the ball was last played by **A**, was in active play and gained an advantage by being in that position.

DIAGRAM 14 – OFF-SIDE

Ball Rebounding from Goal Posts or Crossbar

A shoots for goal and the ball rebounds from the post to **B** who kicks the ball into goal.

The goal is disallowed since **B**, who was in an off-side position when the ball was last played by **A**, was in active play and gained an advantage by being in that position.

DIAGRAM 15 – OFF-SIDE

Corner Kick

A takes a corner kick and the ball goes to **B**.

B shoots for goal and the ball is touched by **C** and enters the goal. The goal is not permitted since **C** was in front of the ball and there were not at least two opponents between him and the goal-line when it was last played by **B**.

DIAGRAM 16 – NOT OFF-SIDE

Corner Kick

A corner kick is taken by **A** and the ball goes to **B** who scores.

Although **B** has only one opponent between him and the goal-line, the goal is allowed since a player cannot be off-side if he receives the ball direct from a corner kick.

DIAGRAM 17 – NOT OFF-SIDE

Throw-in

A throws the ball to B who scores.

The goal is allowed.

Although **B** is in front of the ball and there is only one opponent between him and the goal-line, he is not off-side because a player cannot be offside if he receives the ball direct from a throw-in.

DIAGRAM 18 – NOT OFF-SIDE

Pass to a Team Mate

B plays the ball ahead of A who is in his own half.

Although there are not at least two opponents nearer their own goal-line at the moment when B played the ball, A is not off-side since a player cannot be offside in his own half of the field of play.

DIAGRAM 19(a), (b) – NOT OFF-SIDE

(a) The ball is kicked to the goalkeeper by defender **X**. An attacking player **A** runs towards the goalkeeper to challenge him.

(b) The goalkeeper kicks the ball up-field and the attacking player **A** turns to take up an onside position.

DIAGRAM 19(c) – NOT OFF-SIDE

(c) The ball is intercepted by player **B**, a team mate of the attacking player. It is transferred to another team mate, player **C**, on the wing.

Although the attacking player **A** is in an off-side position, he would not be penalised since he is not involved in active play.

Diagrams illustrating some aspects of SERIOUS FOUL PLAY

The attacker, number 9, is making his way towards goal with an obvious goalscoring opportunity when he is (intentionally) tripped by a defender.

According to Law 12, this would be regarded as serious foul play and the defender must be sent off.

An attacker is making his way towards goal when he is (intentionally) tripped by an opponent. He did not, however, have an obvious goalscoring opportunity.

According to Law 12, this would not be regarded as serious foul play.

3

An attacker making his way to goal with an obvious goalscoring opportunity attempts to move past the goalkeeper who (intentionally) holds him. A penalty kick is awarded.

According to Law 12, this would be regarded as serious foul play and the goalkeeper must be sent off.

4

An attacker is (intentionally) held by the goalkeeper inside the penalty area and a penalty kick is awarded.

The attacker is moving away from goal and so does not have an obvious goalscoring opportunity.

According to Law 12, this would not be regarded as serious foul play.

5

The attacker is (intentionally) tripped inside the penalty area and a penalty kick is awarded. There was, however, no obvious goalscoring opportunity since the player was moving away from goal.

According to Law 12, this would not be regarded as serious foul play.

6

The attacker, number 11, is (intentionally) tripped but there is no obvious goalscoring opportunity since he is not moving towards goal.

According to Law 12, this would not be regarded as serious foul play.

7

An attacker shoots for goal but an outfield player punches the ball over the bar, thus preventing a goal being scored.

According to Law 12, this player is guilty of serious foul play and must be sent off.

If the defender had intentionally punched or handled the ball and the ball had entered the goal he would not have been guilty of serious foul play according to Law 12, but he should be cautioned for ungentlemanly conduct.

8

An attacker, number 10, plays the ball and it is intentionally handled by a defender inside the penalty area. A penalty kick would be awarded.

According to Law 12, this would not be regarded as serious foul play.

If the ball had struck the defender on the hand accidentally no offence would have been committed and play would have been allowed to continue.

The attacker, number 11, is running on to a forward pass and has an obvious goalscoring opportunity. A defender jumps up and deliberately handles the ball thus preventing an obvious goalscoring opportunity.

According to Law 12, this player is guilty of serious foul play and must be sent off.

An attacker is running on to a forward pass with an obvious goalscoring opportunity when the goalkeeper rushes from his goal and intentionally handles the ball outside the penalty area.

According to Law 12, the goalkeeper is guilty of serious foul play and must be sent off.

Videos

Code	Title	Price
	SOCCER TACTICS & SKILLS VIDEOS	
VID001	Attacking in the Attacking 3rd of the Field	£23.44
VID002	Passing & Support	£23.44
VID003	Creating Space	£23.44
VID004	Defending	£23.44
VID005	Defending & Attacking Free Kicks & Corners	£23.44
VID006	Shooting	£23.44
VID007	Goalkeeping	£23.44
VID008	Complete Set – Including a free copy of book	£164.08
	THE WINNING FORMULA VIDEOS	
VID010	Direct Play	£11.99
VID011	Scoring	£11.99
VID012	Winning the Advantage	£11.99
VID013	Defending to Win	£11.99
VID014	Goalkeeping	£11.99
VID015	Complete Set	£49.95
REF001	The Role of the Referee/Fitness Training	£34.66
REF002	Use of the Penalty Mark/Judging Challenges	£34.66
VID020	Soccer Star Video	£10.95

All these video tapes and all publications are available from:–
FA Publications,
9 Wyllyotts Place,
Potters Bar,
Herts. EN6 2JD.

Payment may be made by credit card (Visa/Access/Amex/ Switch)
by telephoning 'FA Publications' on 01707 651840 or
faxing on 01707 644190.

Code	Title	Price
	PUBLICATIONS	
PUB006	Soccer Tactics & Skills	£12.99
PUB007	The Winning Formula	£9.99
PUB019	Coaching & Teaching with Disabilities	£2.95
PUB010	Soccer Star Book	£3.00
PUB018	Soccer Star Challenge Pack	£3.00
NVQ001	Football Curriculum Guide	£9.50
PUB001	FA Diary 1997/98 (Available August '97)	£3.99
PUB002	FA Yearbook 1997/98	£6.99
PUB003	FA Handbook 1997/98	£5.00
PUB011	Laws of Association Football (Ref. Chart)	£5.25
PUB012	Arrangement of Fixtures	£1.00
PUB013	Know The Game Soccer	£3.99
PUB015	Flying Start Soccer (hard cover)	£6.50
PUB016	Flying Start Soccer (soft cover)	£2.95
PUB025	Official Illustrated History of The FA Cup	£25.00
PUB024	Soccer Referee's Manual	£10.99